CONFLICT RESOLUTION

Published by World Teachers Press®
www.worldteacherspress.com

Published with the permission of R.I.C. Publications Pty. Ltd.

First published by R.I.C. Publications Pty. Ltd., Perth, Western Australia. Revised by Didax Educational Resources.

Printed in the United States of America.

Order Number 2-5223
ISBN 978-1-58324-180-6

C D E F G 11 10 09 08 07

395 Main Street
Rowley, MA 01969
www.didax.com

Foreword

Conflict is a part of everyday life. Unfortunately, many people lack the skills to resolve conflict fairly. Teaching students conflict resolution skills can not only turn conflict into a positive experience for everyone involved, it can also create a caring school atmosphere, promote problem-solving skills, and encourage peace.

The practical activities in this book will help students understand how to resolve conflict successfully, and allow them to practice skills and strategies to COMMUNICATE, NEGOTIATE, and CONSOLIDATE conflict resolution procedures.

Titles in this series:

Conflict Resolution, Grades K – 2
Conflict Resolution, Grades 3 – 5
Conflict Resolution, Grades 6 – 8

Contents

Teacher's notes

Each student page is supported by a teacher's page which provides the following information.

Teacher page   **Student page**

Teacher information provides the teacher with detailed additional information to supplement the student page. Teaching points are also included where appropriate.

Discussion points have been suggested to further develop ideas on the student page.

Heading reflects the concept being presented.

The **icon** on each page represents the successful resolution of a conflict situation.

Artwork to introduce or reinforce a conflict scenario.

Specific **indicators** explain what the students are expected to demonstrate through completing the activities.

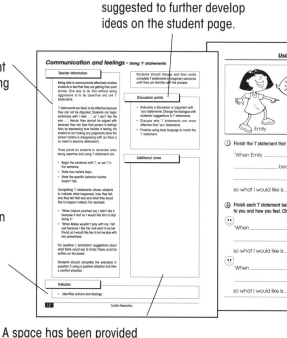

A space has been provided for any **additional notes** the teacher may require, such as reference material or personal information on real-life incidents.

Written student activity to reinforce and develop understanding of the concept.

What is conflict resolution?

Conflict resolution is a process that directs responsibility for solving a conflict to the people involved. Clear steps are followed to achieve a solution that suits both parties. These are:

- defining the problem
- brainstorming possible solutions
- agreeing on the best solution
- putting the best solution into action

In schools, students faced with opposing viewpoints will often go to a teacher to sort out a conflict and decide on a solution. Instead, students should be encouraged to use conflict resolution to resolve minor conflicts such as name-calling, spreading

rumors, taking property without asking, teasing, and invading personal space. The conflict resolution process teaches students that conflict need not be a negative experience, but can motivate change and provide opportunities.

This book helps students to understand conflict resolution steps, comprehend, analyze, and solve conflict resolution scenarios, gain an understanding of the consequences of actions during conflict, and use role-play to problem-solve and identify feelings during conflict.

Teacher's notes

What is peer mediation?

Peer mediation is used when conflicting parties have tried to solve a conflict on their own but cannot agree on a fair solution. A neutral third student is then asked to help.

Peer mediation should only be attempted in a school where staff and students have attended a training course. As not all students have the personality to be effective mediators, students who are to be trained in the process should be chosen carefully.

Peer mediators are trained to:

- use conflict resolution steps to help two people solve a problem
- listen to both sides of the story
- use a consistent approach to solving problems
- be impartial
- attack the problem, rather than the people involved
- encourage the conflicting parties to treat each other with respect

This book helps students to understand mediation steps and how to use compromise and decision making. But at this level, students are NOT expected to be mediators. They will observe the teacher or older students as mediators and learn the steps.

What is negotiation?

Negotiation is the problem-solving process used to resolve conflict. The goal of negotiation is to create a solution the conflicting parties agree to.

Before a negotiation meeting, the people involved should think carefully about what they will say. The parties then meet in a quiet, neutral place; e.g. a "negotiating table" in a corner of the classroom. The conflict is identified and an agreement to resolve it is made.

An important part of the negotiation process is using "I" statements to describe wants and needs. When describing wants and needs, students should speak calmly and give reasons. When listening to someone else, they should demonstrate active listening through positive feedback and eye contact.

Effective negotiation relies on clear communication, problem-solving skills, showing respect, and finding a "win-win" solution.

This book helps students understand the steps that should be used during negotiation, express their needs and wants, and understand what makes a good negotiator.

Focus on the problem,
not the person.

Teacher's notes

What skills and attitudes should be fostered?

For conflict resolution to be effective in a class or school, certain skills and attitudes are necessary. The following skills and attitudes are a focus of the activities in this book.

• Appreciating differences and tolerance

Conflict is often caused by a lack of understanding of others. Tolerance and appreciating differences should therefore be encouraged in students. Tolerance is an on-going process that teaches children not to hate. Teachers can teach tolerance most effectively by modeling tolerant behavior in the classroom and playground, ensuring students are exposed to multicultural literature and images, and teaching them about various faiths, ethnicities, and lifestyles. Educating students to be tolerant will:

- promote the understanding and acceptance of individual differences

- promote the idea that differences can enhance our relationships and enrich our society

- minimize generalizations and stereotyping

- promote the need to combat prejudice and discrimination

A core belief creates blindspots so it's important to really hear the other person's story.

• Communication skills

Speaking and listening skills are vital to prevent and resolve conflicts. Students should be encouraged to speak clearly and calmly and use eye contact, particularly when involved in negotiation. The role-play activities in this book provide students with opportunities to practice these skills. Active listening also needs to be learned and practiced because people involved in conflict often fail to interpret correctly what others are saying.

Students will explore the value of good communication in this book through activities that help them to recognize a good listener and use "I" statements correctly.

Communication is an expression of thought. Barriers such as anger can lead to that communication not being received. It's hard to accept anything from someone when angry. It is important to cushion a person's emotions when negotiating a solution.

• Anger management

It is important for teachers to create an atmosphere in their classrooms that allows students to express and manage angry feelings. This can be done by ensuring that all rules are clear, fair, and consistent, adopting anger management strategies for certain students, and modeling positive anger management strategies such as taking a deep breath, getting away from the situation that is causing the anger, trying to relax, or self-talk.

Students will learn about anger management in this book through activities that help them to recognize suitable and unsuitable reactions to conflict.

Teacher's notes

• Peacemaking

The goal of peacemaking is to ensure that all people are able to fully enjoy their human rights. For students to be effective peace makers, they should have an understanding of what peace is, its importance, and how they can create it. To begin with, they should understand that peace is not a passive state (a lack of war), but a process which relies on communication and action to be created and sustained. Teachers should emphasize resolving conflicts at all levels to reach a peaceful solution where everyone wins.

Students will learn about the value of peace in this book through activities that help them to reflect on what peace means and by finding peaceful solutions to situations.

• Teamwork

The ability to work with others towards a common goal is a vital conflict resolution skill that can be practiced in a range of curriculum areas. The following qualities are necessary for a team to function at its best:

- Working towards a clear goal - The team clearly understands and works towards the goal that is to be achieved.

- Good communication - The team members listen to each other with respect and willingly share their ideas without domination.

- Consideration - The team members encourage and support each other's ideas, giving critical feedback.

Students will learn about teamwork in this book through activities that allow them to participate in team-building, evaluate their teamwork, and discover the qualities of a good team.

• Problem solving

Students should become familiar with problem-solving steps to solve conflict. The following steps should be taught:

- define the problem

- brainstorm possible solutions

- evaluate the ideas

- decide on a solution and carry it out

Students will explore problem solving in this book through activities that require them to use the steps described above.

Teacher's notes

How can conflict resolution be implemented in a classroom or school?

Schools that have implemented conflict resolution programs report that conflicts are being handled more quickly, physical fighting is declining, and more caring behavior is shown.

The first step in implementing conflict resolution programs is to create a cooperative classroom and school environment where rules, rights, and responsibilities are clearly stated, and where students feel able to say what they feel. The school should also hold the belief that social skills are as important as academic skills.

Teachers can also:

- teach or encourage the skills and attitudes covered in "What skills and attitudes should be fostered?"

- inform parents of conflict resolution steps; ask them to support the program by encouraging their children to use conflict resolution steps to solve problems at home

- introduce mediation training courses for students and staff (details of mediation courses can be found on the Internet; try typing "school mediation courses" into a search engine)

- teach students how to deliver "I" statements correctly

- hang charts with conflict resolution steps in the classroom and around the school

- create a "negotiating corner" in the classroom

Glossary

Below are some specialized conflict resolution terms used in this book.

"I" statements

"I" statements tell the way someone feels about a situation, using the word "I" at the beginning of the statement; e.g. "I don't like it when you call me names," "I feel angry when you are always late." "I" statements should be used in the negotiation stage of conflict resolution. They are preferable to a person beginning a sentence with "You …" because this implicitly accuses the other person of causing the problem and decreases the chance of resolution. ("I" statements are also called "'I' messages" in some schools and publications.)

lose-lose

A conflict resolution result in which neither person achieves his or her wants and needs.

mediator

A neutral third party who is called in to help two people in conflict solve the problem themselves.

negotiating table

A quiet area set aside for students to solve conflict.

win-lose

A conflict resolution result in which one person achieves his or her wants and needs but the other person does not.

win-win

A conflict resolution result in which both people at least partially achieve their wants and needs.

Understanding conflict – *What is conflict?*

Teacher information

Conflict between individuals and groups is a part of everyday life. Conflict may be caused by different needs, values or beliefs, prejudice, or limited resources. People may become involved in conflict for a number of reasons. These include the need for justice, retaliation, defense, or to maintain an image. Students may deal with conflict in a variety of ways—avoidance, fighting, fleeing, giving in—which are the least effective ways.

Conflict for younger children involves situations where one or both parties feels angry, upset, confused, or unhappy about what is happening.

To resolve a conflict situation, students should feel comfortable enough to express their feelings, listen to others, and negotiate a solution that suits both parties.

The first priority is to establish a cooperative classroom and school environment where the rules, rights, and responsibilities are clearly stated, and where students feel able to say what they feel. Students should be aware of class rules and their rights and responsibilities.

Discussion points

Page 11 can be used as a stand-alone picture, especially for younger students. Talk with the class as well as using the discussion points below. Alternatively, students can complete the questions on page 13 after the picture talk. Students could also improvise short scenes among the children in the scene.

Students look at the picture and identify situations where a conflict may occur.

- What does conflict mean? Brainstorm other words for conflict; e.g. argument, disagreement.
- How do you think the children feel?
- What is a good solution?
- What is happening in each situation?
- How could each situation lead to conflict?
- How can we prevent conflict?
- What situations have you encountered where there is/was a conflict?
- How did you resolve the situation?
- Did anyone have to help? (Introduce Mom, Dad, teacher as mediator.)

Additional notes

Indicators

- Identifies conflict in everyday situations.
- Recognizes that students may choose to react to a conflict situation in different ways.
- Recognizes that the choice will affect the outcome of the conflict.

Understanding Conflict – *What is conflict?*

Teacher information

Students will need to view the picture on page 11 to complete the activity.

Students need practice identifying conflict situations.

Quite often a conflict may be avoided if students follow basic rules such as taking turns and sharing, and exercising good manners.

Discussion points

- What colors would be used to show conflict?
- What would be appropriate colors to use to show peace?
- What situations cause conflict in your family?
- How do you feel when you argue with your best friend?
- How do you make up?

Additional notes

Indicator

- Views a picture story about conflict situations to answer literal and interpretive comprehension questions.

What is conflict?

Look at the picture on page 11. Answer the questions.

① *What do you think a "conflict" is?* _____

_____

② **In different colors, circle the situations where a conflict may occur.**

③ **Choose one of the possible conflict situations.**

(a) *What is happening?*

_____

_____

_____

_____

_____

(b) *What is the problem?*

_____

_____

_____

_____

_____

(c) *Write how you think the children are feeling.*

(d) *What could they do to fix the problem?*

_____

_____

_____

_____

_____

_____

Understanding conflict – *When I was in a conflict ...*

Teacher information

The situation chosen by the student may have been solved by a mediator (Mom, Dad, teacher, etc.) or resolved in a way where the solution was felt to be unfair to him/her.

Students should discuss various solutions to the problem, even if it wasn't the one used, and also why a certain solution is the best.

Conflict situations occur daily in the classroom and playground. As these occur, the teacher should follow the same steps as a mediator to solve the problem equitably and to serve as a role model to ensure that students are aware of the mediation process.

Discussion points

- Name some situations which cause conflict in the classroom or playground.
- Are there conflicts which occur often in a family situation? If so, what are they?
- Which conflicts often occur between friends?
- What feelings indicate that a situation is a conflict situation?
- How can a solution be reached?

Additional notes

Indicators

- Identifies conflict in everyday situations.
- Identifies the problem, the feelings, the action, and the best solution to a conflict situation.

(1) Draw a picture of a situation where you have been in a conflict.

That's my pencil!

No, it's not!

(2) *What was the problem?*

_____

_____

_____

_____

(3) *How were you feeling?*

(4) *What did you do?*

_____

_____

_____

(5) *Was this the best solution?* (yes) (no)

Why/Why not? _____

_____

Understanding conflict – *Looking at conflicts*

Teacher information

Individuals react differently to situations. Feelings such as anger, sadness, happiness, rejection, and violence are all reactions to a conflict situation. Students should be made aware that these feelings are natural reactions. How they control these feelings is the important aspect. Students need to be aware that most situations can be resolved in a non-violent manner, with a solution that suits both parties (a "win-win" outcome). Behaviors such as teasing, swearing, name-calling, hitting, or shoving are not considered correct solutions. Identifying feelings and anger management will be covered in the following pages.

Discussion points

- Have you ever been in a situation like this? What happened?
- In what ways do people act in these situations? (Include positive and negative solutions.) For example, in picture B the big sister could tell her little sister to go away and leave them alone or they could play together.
- How could the situation get worse? What kind of behavior is worse?
- How could we stop the situation from getting worse?

Additional notes

Indicator

- Identifies different reactions to conflict.

① *What is the problem in each picture?*

(A)_____   (B)_____

_____   _____

_____   _____

② *How do you think these children feel?*

Boy watching cartoons – _____

Boy doing homework – _____

Older sister – _____

Younger sister – _____

③ *What could they do?*

(A) _____   (B) _____

_____   _____

_____   _____

Communication and feelings – *Are you a good listener?*

Teacher information

An important skill used to resolve conflicts is listening. Often, what a person hears and understands is not the message being sent. Listening is vital to all aspects of learning and may be developed in a number of ways. Listening to audio tapes and stories, following directions, listening to instructions and news, and repeating messages all help to develop communication skills.

Many games, such as "Telephone," are useful in developing listening skills.

Students may not know how to listen properly. They should follow steps such as:

• Face the person speaking.

• Keep still and don't fidget.

• Think about what the person is saying.

Listening to and respecting another person's point of view is an important skill contributing to conflict resolution.

Teacher Instructions

Students need colored pencils/crayons for this activity.

Teachers of younger students may ask them to draw their pictures on large sheets of paper without requiring they answer the questions.

(Read each instruction once only. Speak slowly and clearly and allow time for students to complete each instruction.)

1. Draw a big tree in the middle of the box.
2. Put a bird in a nest in the tree.
3. Draw some yellow, red, and orange flowers around the tree.
4. Draw some spikey green grass among the flowers.
5. In the sky, on the left-hand side, draw a flock of birds flying.
6. At the top right-hand side of the box, draw a big sun with a smiley face.
7. Color the sky blue all the way down to the ground.

When students have finished, teachers/helpers can mark each correctly drawn instruction with a check mark. Alternatively, students can swap pictures with a partner and check each correctly drawn instruction after the teacher repeats and clearly explains what should have been drawn. Teachers can also collect the pictures, mark them when convenient and redistribute them for students to complete the bottom section.

Discussion points

• How can you tell if a person is listening to you?
• How can you make it easier for others to listen to you?
• Who do you talk to when you want someone to listen to you?
• What qualities make a good listener?

Indicator

• Listens carefully to instructions to complete an activity.

Are you a good listener?

① Listen carefully to your teacher to draw the picture in the box.

How well did you listen?

② Complete the section below.

I drew $\overline{7}$ parts correctly.

I drew $\overline{7}$ parts incorrectly.

What did she say?

Color the sky blue right to the ground!

③ I heard these words incorrectly._____

_____

④ I am a good listener.

(yes) no)

```
1       2       3       4       5       6       7
|-------|-------|-------|-------|-------|-------|
Practice                                    Great
more!                                       listener!
```

Communication and feelings - *Using "I" statements*

Teacher information

Being able to communicate effectively enables students to feel that they are getting their point across. One way to do this without being aggressive is to be assertive and use "I" statements.

"I" statements are likely to be effective because they cannot be disputed. Students can begin sentences with "I feel …" or "I don't like the way …" Hence, they cannot be argued with because they are how that person is feeling! Also, by expressing how he/she is feeling, the student is not making any judgments about the person he/she is disagreeing with (so there is no need to become defensive!).

Three points for students to remember when being assertive and using "I" statements are:

- Begin the sentence with "I" or use "I" in the sentence.
- State how he/she feels.
- State the specific behavior he/she doesn't like.

Completing "I" statements allows students to indicate what happened, how they felt, why they felt that way, and what they would like to happen instead. For example:

- "When Adrian pinched me, I didn't like it because it hurt so I would like him to stop doing it."
- "When Abbey wouldn't play with me, I felt sad because I like her and want to be her friend, so I would like her to let me play with her sometimes."

For question 1, brainstorm suggestions about what Nina could say to Emily. These could be written on the board.

Students should complete the examples in question 2 using a positive situation and then a conflict situation.

Students should discuss and then orally complete "I" statements to imaginary scenarios until they are familiar with the process.

Discussion points

- Role-play a discussion or argument with "you" statements. Change the dialogue with students' suggestions to "I" statements.
- Discuss why "I" statements are more effective than "you" statements.
- Practice using body language to match the "I" statement.

Additional notes

Indicator

- Identifies actions and feelings.

(1) **Finish the "I" statement that Nina could say about Emily.**

"When Emily _____ I felt

_____ because _____

_____

so what I would like is _____."

(2) **Finish each "I" statement below to show something happening to you and how you feel. Choose a happy and sad thing.**

"When _____ I feel _____

_____ because _____

so what I would like is _____."

"When _____ I feel _____

_____ because _____

so what I would like is _____."

Communication and feelings – *What is the best solution?*

Teacher information

Solutions to conflict situations where neither party is satisfied are unsatisfactory. Neither should one party "win" at the expense of the other. Compromises may be needed. Students need to be aware that each party may not get exactly what he/she wants.

The teacher reads the scenario to the students, then asks them to identify the best solution by putting a checkmark next to it.

Scenario A on page 23 shows a group of boys playing soccer in their favorite place.

Scenario B on page 23 shows a different group of boys playing soccer in the same place.

Scenario C on page 23 shows the boys playing soccer together.

Other solutions may satisfy both parties just as well. For example:

- The boys may decide to play for half an hour and swap places.
- The boys may decide to alternate times to use the soccer field—recess/lunch/ certain days of the week.

Teachers of young students may ask them to listen to the scenario and discuss oral solutions to the conflict.

Discussion points

- Who decides the best solution when conflicts happen at your house?
- Are the solutions fair? Why or why not?
- Describe a conflict situation which was resolved in such a way that you felt that it was an unfair solution.
- Why did you think the solution was unfair?
- Think of "creative solutions" to common conflict situations.

Additional notes

Indicator

- Identifies the best solution to a conflict situation.

What is the best solution?

Jason and his two friends, Thomas and Luke, were going to the playground to play soccer. Shamal, Jack, and Sam also wanted to play there. Shamal had brought his new soccer ball especially to use that day. Both groups wanted to use the same part of the playground for their game.

① What is the best solution? Put a checkmark next to it.

② Can you think of another solution?

_____

_____

_____

③ Was the solution fair for both groups? _____

Why/Why not? _____

_____

_____

Communication and feelings – *How would you feel? – 1*

Teacher information

Students need to be aware that body language, such as facial features, stance, and position, is a key to how a person is feeling.

Students should practice displaying and reading facial expressions—happy, sad, scared, angry, worried, etc.

Students will choose and color the appropriate facial expression representing the emotion they would feel in each conflict situation.

Scenario 1 on page 25 shows a child waiting to go home from school. All the other children have been picked up. He is beginning to worry.

Scenario 2 on page 25 shows a child wanting to join in a game. The other children do not want her to be a part of the game.

Scenario 3 on page 25 shows two children walking home from school, when they are confronted by a bigger, older child. They are feeling a bit worried and scared.

Scenario 4 on page 25 shows two students making masks. One student bumps the other while she is trying to work. She is feeling upset because she accidentally painted the wrong part of her mask.

Scenario 5 on page 25 shows a child who is late for class. She is feeling worried or anxious.

Scenario 6 on page 25 shows two students fighting over the last sheet of paper. The student on the left is feeling angry.

Discussion points

- During shared reading times, view and discuss facial expressions depicting the feelings of a character from the book.
- Brainstorm types of feelings with the students and display a face depicting each emotion (the faces on page 25 may be enlarged for this use).
- List situations when students feel each emotion. Some situations may cover more than one emotion; e.g. birthday party – happy, excited.
- What is happening in each picture in the worksheet? How do you think that person feels?

Additional notes

Indicator

- Matches facial expressions depicting feelings to pictures showing conflict situations.

Look at the pictures. Color the face which shows how **you** would feel if this was happening to you.

Communication and feelings – *How would you feel? - 2*

Teacher information

Different situations evoke different emotions. Students should be aware that each of us reacts to different situations in different ways.

Students should complete the table and be confident in expressing their feelings in everyday situations.

Discussion points

- What makes you happy? Sad? Worried? Excited?
- Discuss situations where most students feel the same emotion. For example, waking on his/her birthday would elicit happiness or excitement from most students.
- Categorize situations by the feelings felt, for example:

Happiness
cooking with Nanna
going on a trip
visit from cousins
Christmas Day
birthday

Sadness
rejected by friend
favorite toy lost
friend moving away
death of a pet

Additional notes

Indicator:

- Identifies feelings to match a situation.

How would you feel? – 2

Describe how you would feel if each thing happened to you.

What happened	How I would feel
I got a birthday gift from my best friend.	I would feel happy and pleased.
My big brother hit me.	I would feel _____
I went on the big jungle gym for the first time.	I would feel _____
My dad told funny jokes.	I would feel _____
I got all my spelling words right.	I would feel _____
I joined a new soccer team.	I would feel _____
My best friend teased me.	I would feel _____
My pet fish died.	I would feel _____

Communication and feelings – *Positive and negative feelings*

Teacher information

Even very young students can be taught simple conflict resolution skills. Early personal development activities such as building self-esteem, understanding types of feelings, respecting similarities and differences among peers (empathy), and anger management contribute to the development of conflict resolution skills.

Students should be aware that not all feelings are good, but are a normal part of life. Everyone experiences feelings of lack of self-esteem or confidence, anger, jealousy, etc. at some time or another. How we deal with these feelings is the important thing. Non-violent solutions are the basis of conflict resolution.

Teachers of very young students may wish to discuss situations rather than ask students to complete page 29.

Discussion points

- Discuss situations when you have felt angry, worried, jealous, excited, sad, happy.
- Identify negative (bad) and positive (good) feelings.
- How do you act when you get angry? What do you do?
- What makes you feel happy? Sad?
- What things do you worry about?

Additional notes

Indicators

- Identifies negative and positive feelings.
- Identifies situations that evoke negative and positive feelings.

1 **Draw a picture and complete the sentence.**

I feel angry when _____ _____

I feel jealous when _____ _____

I feel worried when _____ _____

I feel sad when _____ _____

I feel happy when _____ _____

I feel excited when_____ _____

2 **Color** ☺ **or** ☹ **to show if each feeling is positive or negative.**

Communication and feelings – *What makes me angry?*

Teacher information

Teachers of young students may wish to discuss situations that cause anger and emphasize the steps for dealing with anger.

Use the poem on page 31 as a stimulus for discussing feelings of anger.

Suggested steps for anger management:

> Walk away.
> Count to 10.
> Do not lose another friend!

Suggest to students to take calming breaths, keep their hands to themselves, and not say anything nasty back—all these actions help to defuse a volatile situation.

Discussion points

- Discuss the situations in the poem that caused the boy to feel angry (mad).
- What makes you angry?
- What can you do when you get angry?
- How can you stop being angry?
- How can you help a friend who is angry?

Additional notes

Indicator

- Identifies feelings of anger and things that cause anger.

What makes me angry?

Read the poem about this person's day.

A Very Mad Bad Day

My brother hit me,

So I got mad.

My dog bit me,

So I got mad.

The book fell on me,

So I got mad.

Tom told on me,

So I got mad.

I've had a very mad bad day!

I get angry when _____

_____

_____

When I get angry I _____

_____

_____

Write three ways to control your anger.

_____

_____

_____

Team building – *What makes a good team?*

Teacher information

For conflict resolution skills to be taught effectively, a classroom should work as a cooperative unit, with rules, rights, and responsibilities established. Young students thrive on having the responsibility of easy jobs to complete as part of the class "team." This will develop confidence and self-esteem. Good team members:

- listen to each other
- cooperate
- have clear team goals
- allow each member to freely express his/her opinion

Many games such as "Sculptures" and "Shapes," where students have to work in a group to form a given shape (e.g. rowing boat or television), reinforce the concept that team members depend on each other for the whole team to work well.

Discussion points

- Brainstorm types of teams/groups and their goals.
- Discuss jobs/responsibilities in various teams, such as firefighters, schools.

Additional notes

Indicators

- Identifies teams.
- Recognizes characteristics of a good team.
- Recognizes characteristics of a good team member.

What makes a good team?

1 **List three teams that work well. For example, sports team, firefighters, family.**

_____

_____

_____

2 **Answer the questions.**

What do these "teams" need to do to work properly?

_____

_____

_____

How can you be a good team member?

_____

_____

_____

How could you be a good team leader or what does a good leader do?

_____

_____

_____

Team building – A family is a team

Teacher information

Families usually operate as a team. Each member of the team has a job to do, to help the team work as a whole unit. If one team member does not complete his/her job, the other team members are disadvantaged.

In many families, one or two people take more responsibility than others. This can lead to dissatisfaction and anger. Cooperation makes it easier for all team members and helps to establish a positive team atmosphere.

There are many single-parent families. Children need to be made aware that they can help out by taking on some simple tasks such as taking out the trash or hanging up towels.

Discussion points

- Discuss different types of families.
- Discuss similarities and differences among families.
- Brainstorm ideas for "easing the load" for overburdened family team members.
- Discuss "extended," "blended," and "step" families.

Additional notes

Indicators

- Identifies members of the family "team" and their responsibilities.
- Understands how team members work together.

A family is a team

A family is a team.
Everyone has to help the team work.
Most team members have a job to do.

Complete the chart below to show how your family works together.

Family member	Drawing	Responsibilities/Jobs
_____		
_____		
_____		
_____		
_____		
_____		

What would happen if family members didn't do their jobs?

_____

Team building – Who do you share things with?

Teacher information

Students should be aware that when they have problems, need to share good news, want someone to talk, to etc., they usually choose a certain person (or a small group of people). Good team members listen to each other. Listening is an important team-building skill.

Teachers should make themselves available to students when necessary. Class members should feel comfortable and confident enough to share problems/successes with their own teacher.

Discussion points

- Discuss different reactions to different feelings. For example, some people get angry when they are worried; some like to be alone when they are sad.
- Construct a drawing of a network of people to approach to discuss a problem.

Additional notes

Indicators

- Identifies specific individuals to go to when needed.
- Identifies different people for different purposes.

Who do you share things with?

1. **Complete the sentences below.**

   (a) When I am hurt, I go to _____

   _____

   (b) When I have good news, I tell _____

   (c) When I am sad, I talk to _____

   (d) When Dad is mad, he _____

   _____

   (e) When Dad is happy, he _____

   _____

2. **Complete one for yourself.**

   When _____ is _____,

   _____

3. **Using the balloons below, draw pictures, and label the people you like to share things with.**

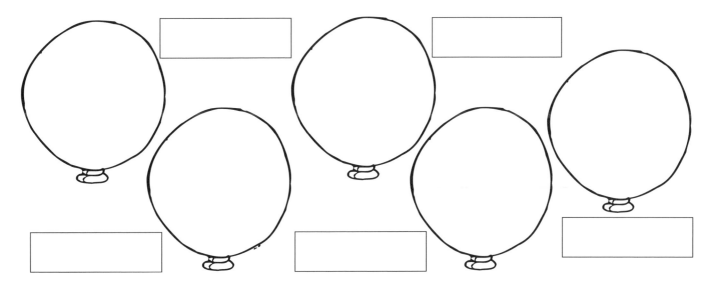

Team building – *We are all different*

We live in a multicultural society. We look different and we live differently. We have different types of families. Differences can enhance our relationships and our society. Students need to be encouraged to recognize, appreciate, and tolerate differences.

Tolerance is a skill which can reduce conflict and the need for conflict resolution. It should be an ongoing process. Tolerance is also a quality needed in team building.

Young children may look for basic physical differences such as hair and eye color or the number of people in the family, types of single parent families, parents born in a different country, both parents working or moms and dads with similar jobs.

Discussion points

- Why do some people look different?
- Why do some people look the same?
- What foods do you eat that come from another country?
- Who was born in the United States? Who was born in another country?
- Are there any traditions/customs that you follow in your family?

Additional notes

Indicators

- Identifies differences and similarities among people.
- Recognizes that students who are different are not better/worse.
- Recognizes that we must tolerate differences.

We are all different

① **Complete the table below.**

	Me	My best friend
age		
hair color		
eye color		
height		
weight		
number of family members		
address		

② **Write two things that are the same.** _____

_____

③ **Write two things that are different.** _____

_____

Draw your best friend.

④ *Why do you like your best friend?*

_____

_____

Team building – *What do you think they look like? – 1*

Teacher information

As individuals, we quite often have preconceived ideas about people. We feel comfortable grouping people in recognizable, easy-to-handle stereotypes. Very often, our ideas do not correlate with the actual person.

- Stereotypes are fixed ideas we have about people or animals. They are conventional ideas that society places on groups with the same attitudes, interests, characteristic traits, or physical features.
- Stereotypes are reinforced by the media as shortcuts to creating characters or as a quick means of communicating ideas effectively.
- Stereotypes:
  - ~ can change
  - ~ should be questioned as to the role they play
  - ~ should lead to discussion of other possible alternatives for representing the character/group
- Students will understand this concept more after completing the activity on page 41. Compare their drawings with others in the class and those given in Question 2. Learning not to make assumptions and being open-minded is another important quality in team building. Conflicts can occur if we make assumptions about stereotypes.
- Television and other media forms constantly bombard us with stereotypes. Advertisements in books and magazines encourage us to classify people in similar ways. Students need to be aware of stereotypes as they are used to sell certain products.

Discussion points

- Brainstorm groups of people different from the students. Why and how are they different?
- Brainstorm types of jobs now done by both men and women; e.g. members of the armed services.
- Students select a type of person and write a description. Examples may include a 50-year-old, a security guard, a firefighter, or a teenager.
- Discuss and compare the descriptions. (A student may have a 50-year-old grandfather who is fit, active, and has a challenging job, but his/her description of a 50-year-old may involve grey hair, walking cane, etc.)

Additional notes

Indicator

- Recognizes that we should not make assumptions about people.

① **Draw a picture to match the description.**

Description	Drawing
(a) Robert goes to school with his friends. He learns to read, write, and do math. He likes to play at lunchtime.	
(b) Georgia's mom goes to work every day. She works very hard. She wears a uniform and meets lots of people.	

Look at the pictures below and answer the questions.

② Would these pictures match the descriptions above? (yes) (no)

Why/Why not? _____

_____

Did either of your pictures match these pictures? (yes) (no)

Team building – *What do you think they look like? - 2*

Teacher information

Students should view each picture and draw alongside a person or a character who can do the job or role but is not a stereotype.

Discuss who these may be and the characteristics of the person or character in each picture. Encourage the students to think of atypical stereotypes. For the examples given, students may come up with the following suggestions.

- ~ Super Ant/Banana Man or other cartoon character
- ~ active older lady, jogging, swimming or playing golf
- ~ house husband/housekeeper
- ~ young sophisticated woman in a nice suit with a briefcase
- ~ well-dressed, attractive young woman

- The activity on page 43 will further develop students' understanding of the concept of stereotypes and the importance of not making assumptions about people, learning tolerance and team building and how all these qualities help prevent conflict.

Discussion points

- What is a stereotype? (Stereotypes are fixed ideas we have about people etc.)
- What stereotypes have you seen on TV?
- Discuss symbols used to identify a character/ stereotype; e.g. clothes, physical appearance, setting.

Additional notes

Indicator

- Identifies typical stereotypes and atypical stereotypes.

Look at the pictures below. In the empty boxes, draw a picture of a person or character who does the same job but does not look the same as the drawing. The first one is done for you. If you have seen one on TV, or know one, write the name next to the drawing.

① superhero		Super Dog
② movie star		_____
③ grandparent		_____
④ housecleaner		_____
⑤ business person		_____
⑥ rock star		_____

Conflict resolution skills – *Steps for resolving a conflict*

Teacher information

Pages 47 – 52 are to be used in conjunction with each other.

The steps on page 45 need to be followed to achieve a fair, win-win solution to a conflict.

The students should practice saying the exact words in order to become familiar with the steps.

The steps on page 45 can be enlarged for display.

Page 47 includes scenarios to be discussed and solved using the conflict resolution steps on page 45.

Students should write their solutions on page 49.

Discussion points

- When do you use steps to complete an activity? Give examples.
- Do specific steps help? How?
- Explain each conflict resolution step.
- Why do different problems cause different feelings in different people?
- Are some feelings common? Why?

Additional notes

Indicator

- Reads and discusses the steps for resolving conflicts.

Steps for resolving a conflict

1 What is the problem? How do you feel?

2 How can we fix the problem?

3 Brainstorm ways to fix the problem.

4 Choose the best option.

5 Agree on the final solution.

Conflict resolution skills – *Conflict resolution scenarios – 1*

Teacher information

Pages 47 – 52 should be used in conjunction with each other. The students should read/listen to the scenarios on page 48 and, using conflict resolution steps, decide on the best solution.

The solution should be the best for both parties.

Discuss all the steps slowly and carefully.

Teachers may wish to give a copy of the scenarios to each student or group of two, enlarge one copy to display, or read the scenarios to the students and discuss.

Allow time for the students to relate similar situations that they have encountered and the solutions they used.

Discussion points

- How many of the conflict situations on page 50 have happened to you?
- How did you feel?
- What did you do?
- Was the conflict resolved in a satisfactory manner?
- Were all parties happy with the situation?
- Were there other solutions that may not have been considered?

Additional notes

Indicator

- Reads and discusses conflict resolution scenarios.

Read the problems below and find the best solution.

Scenario 1

Jeff is sitting on a seat under a tree to eat his lunch. Ethan runs back past the spot where Jeff is sitting. As he does, he knocks Jeff's drink onto the ground. Jeff is upset.

What should the boys do?

Scenario 2

Rebecca and Alyssa are playing in the sandpit together. Aimee and Sjaan would also like to play in the sand. All the shovels and pails are being used.

What should the girls do?

Scenario 3

Tom is walking to the sports playground with some friends to play soccer. He is surprised to see his best friend, Brendan, already playing with another group of boys.

What should the boys do?

Conflict resolution skills – *Evaluating solutions – 1*

Teacher information

A vital step in developing appropriate conflict resolution skills is an evaluation of the process.

Students should be able to evaluate:

- Was the solution the best?
- Was the solution fair/just?
- Were both parties happy with the solution?
- Were there other solutions that weren't considered? (Other students may suggest more creative alternatives.)

Discussion points

- What is similar and different among the students' evaluations of the scenarios?
- Give examples of other activities where an evaluation is needed; for example, following a cooking procedure or a science experiment.
- Why is an evaluation useful? Does it help you to make better decisions next time?

Additional notes

Indicator

- Identifies and evaluates solutions to resolve conflicts.

Complete the questions below.

Scenario 1

What's the solution? _____

Evaluation. (Was this a good solution? Why/Why not?)

_____

Scenario 2

What's the solution? _____

Evaluation. (Was this a good solution? Why/Why not?)

Scenario 3

What's the solution? _____

Evaluation. (Was this a good solution? Why/Why not?)

Conflict resolution skills – *Conflict resolution scenarios – 2*

Teacher information

Pages 50 – 53 should be used in conjunction with each other. The students should read/listen to the scenarios on page 51 and, using conflict resolution steps, decide on the best solution.

Solutions should be the best for both parties.

Discuss all the steps slowly and carefully.

Teachers may wish to give a copy of the scenarios to each student or group of two, enlarge one copy to display, or read the scenarios to the students and discuss.

Allow time for students to relate similar situations that they have encountered and the solutions they used.

Discussion points

- Have you encountered conflict situations similar to those on page 51? If so, what were they? How were they resolved? Were all parties satisfied with the solution?
- Did you follow specific steps to reach a solution?
- Did any adults help to resolve the situation? If so, who and why?

Additional notes

Indicator

- Reads and discusses conflict resolution scenarios.

Read the problems below and find the best solution.

Scenario 4

Mom was visiting Grandma, who was sick. Dad was taking Jessica and Katelyn to the beach. Jessica, who was 10, wanted to sit in the front seat next to Dad. Katelyn, who was eight, wanted to sit there, too. They began to argue.

What is the problem? What could they do?

Scenario 5

Michael and Juan had just finished playing a hard game of basketball. They raced to their bags where they had left their drinks.

"Hey, that's my drink!" said Juan

"No, it's not! It's mine!" said Michael.

"I left it next to my bag!"

What is the problem?
What could they do?

Scenario 6

The twins, Zoe and Amy, arrived home from school and grabbed their work from their bags. They had both done really well at school that day; Zoe got a gold sticker on her reading worksheet and Amy got all her spelling words correct. They rushed through the kitchen door, pushing and shoving to be the first to show Mom their work.

What is the problem? What could they do?

Conflict resolution skills – *Evaluating solutions – 2*

Complete the sections below.

Scenario 4

What's the solution? _____

_____

Evaluation. (Was this a good solution? Why/Why not?)

_____

_____

Scenario 5

What's the solution? _____

_____

Evaluation. (Was this a good solution? Why/Why not?)

_____

_____

Scenario 6

What's the solution? _____

_____

Evaluation. (Was this a good solution? Why/Why not?)

_____

_____

Problem solving – *Problem-solving steps*

Teacher information

Conflict resolution strategies encompass skills such as problem solving in which both parties express how they feel, what they want to happen, and find solutions which satisfy them.

Teaching problem-solving strategies through discussion and role-playing will assist students in learning and developing skills for positive social behaviors and relationships.

When students develop these skills, conflicts will be minimized or resolved in nonviolent ways.

The processes (steps) for problem solving follow steps similar to those for conflict resolution.

Pages 55 to 59 should be used in conjunction with each other. Students should write their solutions on page 59.

Teachers of young students may read the scenarios on page 57 and discuss the best solutions.

Discussion points

- Discuss real-life problems and the solutions as they occur.
- Compare problem-solving number activities.
- Role-play solutions to the scenarios on page 57.
- List occasions when "good" problems occur; for example, choosing between two fun outings, or how to spend a specific amount of pocket money.
- How do these "good" problems make you feel?

Additional notes

Indicator

- Reads and discusses problem-solving steps.

Problem-solving steps

1 What is the problem?

2 What can we do?

3 Did we fix it?

Problem solving – *Problem-solving scenarios*

Teacher information

Everyone is different. We do things in different ways and we often want different things. Sometimes we don't agree with other people and problems are created.

Students encounter problems every day, whether individually or with other students.

Students should follow these simple rules for solving a problem:

• Try to solve problems so that everyone wins.

• Let people know how you feel.

• Listen to how other people feel.

• Say sorry if you hurt someone's feelings.

• Be fair to everyone.

Teachers may read the scenarios on page 57 to young students and discuss them. Older students may read and discuss them with a partner or in small groups. Students may work individually to find solutions to the problems.

Discussion points

• Relate some situations where you have had to say "sorry."

• Discuss some situations where you may have hurt someone's feelings.

• Do other people, including adults, ever say things that may hurt another person's feelings? How do they fix these problems?

• Introduce the concepts of "compromise" and "negotiate." What do these mean?

Additional notes

Indicator

• Reads and discusses problem-solving scenarios.

Problem-solving scenarios

Read the scenarios below and discuss each problem.

Scenario 1

Jordan is walking back from the school cafeteria after buying a popsicle. An older boy in front of him is putting his change back into his wallet after buying some chips. He rushes to meet his friends but does not notice a quarter fall out of his wallet. Jordan spies the coin on the ground and picks it up.

What is the problem? What should he do?

Scenario 2

Natalie is practicing her dancing in the living room when she accidentally knocks Mom's pottery bowl onto the floor, where it cracks.

What is the problem? What should she do?

Scenario 3

Jason and Tyson are in the same class. Declan is a year older and is in a different class. Jason is getting ready to line up after lunch when he notices Declan with his hand in Tyson's bag.

What is the problem? What should he do?

Problem solving – *Evaluating problem-solving solutions*

Teacher information

Students continue to learn and grow by evaluating the steps they have taken to solve a problem.

Students should be able to evaluate:

- What was the problem? (Students may find a number of problems to solve in one scenario.)
- Were there other solutions not used? (Other students may suggest more creative alternatives.)
- Was the solution just/fair?
- Was everyone happy with the solution? (Some scenarios may require students to admit to a wrongdoing and accept their punishment.)

Discussion points

- Praise students who admit to a wrongdoing and accept their punishment. Discuss how it feels to admit to a mistake or to apologize to another person. How do you feel afterwards?
- Discuss punishments imposed in class or at school for various wrongdoings. Why are punishments imposed? Are they fair/just?
- Discuss situations where students are rewarded for correct behavior. How do you feel when you are rewarded for doing the right thing?

Additional notes

Indicator

- Identifies and evaluates problem-solving solutions.

Evaluating problem-solving solutions

Complete the questions below.

Scenario 1

What's the solution? _____

_____

Evaluation. (Was this the best solution? Why/Why not?)

_____

_____

Scenario 2

What's the solution? _____

_____

Evaluation. (Was this the best solution? Why/Why not?)

_____

_____

Scenario 3

What's the solution? _____

_____

Evaluation. (Was this the best solution? Why/Why not?)

_____

_____

Negotiation – *Negotiation steps*

Teacher information

For a successful conflict resolution, students need to negotiate a solution which satisfies both parties.

This will involve listening to each other's point of view, discussion, and compromise before selecting a viable solution. The resolution should be fair and just and be a "win-win" solution for both parties.

Students should use "I" statements (see pages 20 to 21) to explain what happened, how they feel, and what they want the other party to do.

Encourage students to be assertive enough to express their point of view. Assertive people respect others and themselves equally.

Students need to think about what is important and how the other person feels.

They should listen to other people's ideas, find the best solution, and stick with it.

A positive atmosphere should exist for negotiation to take place. Students should feel safe, comfortable, and respected, trusting the mediator to be fair. Students should feel free to give ideas in a polite manner.

The mediator (teacher) should give a brief summary of both points of view, the solution reached and witness the agreement of both parties to the best solution. A handshake may seal the bargain to show agreement.

It is important to note that the best solution for a conflict will involve one or both parties not obtaining exactly what they want. Negotiation should always finish on a positive note. This may simply involve the teacher praising the students for negotiating well and reaching a solution.

Pages 60 – 65 are to be used in conjunction with each other.

Discussion points

- What does "negotiation" mean? Discuss various meanings.
- Why is listening important to negotiation?
- What does "win-win" mean?
- Revise the use of "I" statements. Practice using them correctly.
- Role-play being assertive in various scenarios.

Additional notes

Indicator

- Reads and discusses negotiation steps.

Negotiation steps

1 I say what happened, what I feel and what I want.

2 I listen to the other person do the same. I don't interrupt!

3 We brainstorm solutions to suit us both.

4 We decide on the best solution.

5 We agree to accept this solution.

6 We shake hands.

Negotiation – *Negotiation scenarios*

Teacher information

Pre-negotiation skills may be taught from school entry. As students learn and develop skills for positive social behaviors and relationships, the need for a conflict resolution decreases.

The following is a list of positive social behaviors to be taught, reinforced, and encouraged:

- self-esteem
- awareness of own and others' feelings
- empathy (respecting diversity and difference in others)
- anger management/self-control
- communication
- listening
- searching for solutions (problem solving)
- taking responsibility for own actions

All learning areas provide opportunities for learning and practicing these skills.

Pages 60 to 65 are to be used in conjunction with each other.

Discuss what could happen in the scenarios if the students did not negotiate.

Teachers of young students may read the scenarios on page 63, discuss the solutions and decide on the best one.

Older students can use the template on page 65 to make a written copy of the discussions and solutions of each scenario.

Discussion points

- Encourage self-esteem in the classroom at all times. Play games such as choosing a particular student and having the others list one good thing about that person. For example, Sarah has nice, shiny hair; Jackson is a good runner, etc.
- Students list as many good qualities of their own as they can. Compare and discuss with others.
- Discuss the meaning of "empathy." "How would you feel if this happened to you?"

Additional notes

Indicator

- Reads and discusses negotiation scenarios.

Negotiation scenarios

Read the scenarios below and discuss each problem.

Scenario 1

Ben and Rhyce finally had their names called out by the aide to do their art. It seemed like they had been waiting forever. When they reached the table, there was only one sheet of art paper left. They both wanted the last piece.

What's the problem? What's the best solution?

Scenario 2

Gina and Rebecca are busily completing a worksheet for their portfolio. The teacher wants the work done neatly and correctly using the right colors. Gina has misplaced her brown pencil. The one on Rebecca's table looks exactly like hers. She takes it from Rebecca's table.

What's the problem? What's the best solution?

Scenario 3

Amanda and her brother David have just moved to a new school. Amanda loves to play soccer. She was the best player on her old team. Bryce is in her new class at school. At lunch break, she approaches Bryce and his friends and asks to join in the game. They are very surprised that she would dare to ask to join their game.

What's the problem? What's the best solution?

Negotiation – *Negotiation scenario solutions*

Teacher information

When discussing the scenarios, students may quickly see the obvious solution to a conflict. It is advisable to discuss a number of solutions so students are aware that the wrong solution may lead to an escalation of the conflict.

Negotiation prevents a conflict from developing into non-peaceful actions.

Students need to learn to be objective when discussing scenarios. They need to look at both sides of the conflict to decide what each party wants. Empathy can be a very difficult concept for young children to grasp.

Older students can use the template on page 65 to make a written copy of the discussions and solutions of each scenario.

Discussion points

- Discuss the scenarios on page 63. Relate any similar incidents which may have happened to you.
- How would you feel if this happened to you?
- What is the problem?
- What could you do?
- What are some solutions?

Additional notes

Indicator

- Identifies and evaluates negotiation scenarios.

Complete the questions below.

| Scenario ___ | *What do they want?* |

Name_____   Name _____

_____   _____

_____   _____

_____   _____

Solutions • _____

_____

• _____

_____

• _____

_____

Best solution _____

_____

_____

Draw a picture of the solution.

Mediation – *Mediation steps*

Teacher information

Mediation is the process where a third, neutral party listens to both sides to resolve a conflict. For young students, the mediator (and role model) is the teacher. At a later stage, older students may take on the role of peer mediator after a period of training and practice. (The skill of peer mediation is dealt with in more detail in the upper levels of Conflict Resolution.)

Conflict Resolution, Grades K - 2 deals mostly with pre-mediation skills and relies solely on the teacher as role model to reinforce the steps.

Students may role-play the task of mediator with teacher support but will not take on the actual role. Many programs recommend that students practice the skills of mediation for at least one year before taking on the role.

Mediators must attack the problem rather than the people involved. They encourage the parties to treat each other with respect. During the discussion, each person is required to state the problem, describe his/her feelings, and say how he/she is responsible for the problem. Possible solutions are then brainstormed and a fair solution, suiting both parties, is reached.

Mediation steps follow a similar format to those for negotiation and conflict resolution.

Pages 66 to 71 are to be used in conjunction with each other.

Discussion points

- What does "mediation" mean?
- What does a mediator do?
- Name some adults who act as mediators; for example, Mom, Dad, teacher.
- What are the qualities needed to be a good mediator?

Additional notes

Indicator

- Reads and discusses the mediation steps.

Mediation steps

1 Agree that a solution is needed.

 **2** Listen to both points of view.

3 Discuss the problem.

 **4** Brainstorm solutions.

5 Decide on the best solution.

 **6** Agree on a solution.

7 Summarize the process.

Mediation – *Mediation scenarios*

Teacher information

A good mediator:

- is trained to help two people solve a problem
- does not judge anyone's behavior
- listens to both sides of the story
- uses a consistent approach to solving problems
- is impartial (does not "play favorites")

Teachers of young students may read the scenarios (on page 69) to them and discuss the problem and the best solution using mediation steps.

Older students may complete the sections on page 71, following the steps.

Mature students, under teacher guidance, may role-play being the mediator while other class members observe.

Young students find it difficult to be objective, since they often want the student they like best to have the best result for a solution to a conflict.

Older students can use the template on page 71 to make a written copy of the discussions and solutions of each scenario.

Discussion points

- Name an adult who is a good mediator.
- What skills does this adult display?
- Do you have the qualities to be a good mediator?
- Why do you think so?
- What does "impartial" mean?
- Why is being a good listener important?

Additional notes

Indicator

- Reads and discusses the mediation scenarios.

Read the scenarios below and discuss each problem.

Scenario 1

Dylan was playing baseball with his friends. Ryan was the umpire. Dylan was called out but disagreed with the result. He did not want to give the bat to the next batter.

What's the problem? What are the solutions? What is the best solution?

Scenario 2

Mrs. White had taken her class to the library. She read them a funny book about dogs. When she had finished, she asked her class, "Who would like to borrow the book to take home?" Melissa and Sophie both put up their hands at the same time.

What's the problem? What are the solutions? What is the best solution?

Scenario 3

Tom's mom had taken him to the barber. The next day his mom had spiked his hair with gel just like the barber had. Tom was very proud of his new haircut.

When he got to school, Stevie pointed to his head, laughing and teasing him.

What's the problem? What are the solutions? What is the best solution?

Mediation – Mediation scenario solutions

Teacher information

Bullying causes conflict.

Verbal bullying may include name-calling, making offensive remarks, or insulting someone.

Emotional bullying may include spreading rumors/nasty stories, making fun of someone, or excluding, ignoring, ostracizing, or alienating others. Often, these forms of bullying can be more hurtful and insidious.

People bully for many reasons:

- They may feel upset or angry or feel they don't fit in.
- They want to seem tough or show off.
- They may be bullied themselves by family members.
- They're scared of getting picked on so do it first.
- If they don't like themselves they may take it out on others.
- They think they will become more popular.

Additional activities dealing with bullying may be found in the Bullying series, published by World Teachers Press.

Older students can use the template on page 71 to make a written copy of the discussions and solutions of each scenario.

Discussion points

- Allow students to relate situations similar to those on page 69 that they may have encountered.
- Using other scenarios, discuss solutions to conflict situations.
- Role-play being a mediator in conflict situations.
- Discuss the steps in the mediation process. Repeat the steps in your own words.

Additional notes

Indicator

- Identifies and evaluates mediation scenarios.

Complete the sentences below by using the mediation steps.

Scenario _____

① The problem is _____

_____

_____

② (a)_____ wants _____
        name

_____

(b)_____ wants _____
        name

_____

③ Some solutions are _____

_____

④ The best solution is _____

_____

⑤ The problem is solved because _____

_____

Draw a picture of the solution.

Decision making – Decision-making scenarios

Teacher Information

Deciding on an option that is best for both parties may be difficult. Students should practice making decisions for themselves and accepting the consequences of making those decisions.

At times, students may make the wrong decisions and must learn to live with some failures. An adult or teacher should be able to help if they are asked by a student.

Teachers may read the scenarios on page 65 to young students and discuss the problems orally.

Older students may read the scenarios themselves and complete the worksheet.

Scenario 1 on page 73 indicates a student having to choose between doing homework and riding her bike.

Scenario 2 on page 73 indicates a student having to choose between spraypainting his hair like his friend or feeling silly.

Scenario 3 on page 73 indicates a student having to choose between playing with her friend or jumping on the trampoline.

Students should be aware that some decisions may hurt other people or their feelings.

Discussion points

- Students relate situations where they need to choose between two options.
- Is it easy to do what is fair, rather than what you would like to do? Why?
- Why is it necessary to choose a fair solution?
- Discuss situations where the students know that they have made the wrong decision. What happened? Did they try to fix the problem? If so, how?
- Who or what influences your opinion? Why? How?

Additional notes

Indicator

- Reads and discusses decision-making scenarios.

Decision-making scenarios

Read the scenarios and complete the sentences below.

Scenario 1

I have some reading and spelling to do for homework but I really want to go outside and ride my bike.

I have decided to _____

_____

because _____

Scenario 2

What if I look funny!

My best friend Bryan wants me to spray-paint my hair red for field day but I don't want to look funny.

I have decided to _____

_____

because _____

Scenario 3

Jessica invited me to play at her house this afternoon after school but, today, Sarah also asked me to go to her house to see her new trampoline.

I have decided to _____

_____

because _____

Compromising – *Compromising scenarios*

Teacher information

Compromising is the settling of a problem or argument by both sides agreeing to give way a bit from what each really wants.

Compromising is a difficult skill for young children. They can be egotistical and want the best result for themselves or their best friends.

Learning to compromise is a very important step towards resolving conflicts. Putting themselves in the position of another person helps them to see a solution that will be beneficial to both parties.

Teachers of young students may read the scenarios (page 75) to them and discuss the compromise reached.

Older students should choose one compromise for each scenario and complete the sentences.

Discussion points

- What does "compromise" mean?
- Encourage compromise by asking, "How do you think the other person feels?"
- Students relate conflict situations similar to those on page 75.

Additional notes

Indicator

- Reads and discusses scenarios dealing with compromise.

Compromising scenarios

Read the scenarios and complete the sentences below.

Scenario 1

Jamie wants to play rockstars but Michelle wants to play gymnastics.

They could compromise by _____

_____

_____

Scenario 2

Taryn and her brother Brett have jobs to do at home. Brett has a big project due the next day and he wants to give it his best. He won't have time to do his jobs so he asks Taryn to do them for him.

They could compromise by _____

_____

_____

Scenario 3

Peter and James get a new computer. After school they both want to play with it.

They could compromise by _____

_____

_____

Peace – *What is peace?*

Teacher information

When conflict is resolved, peaceful classrooms, schools, communities, and countries should be evident.

Individuals define the concept of peace in their own way.

Students may find it difficult to put into words what it means to be peaceful or in a peaceful situation. They may find it easier to define peacefulness as an absence of conflict—no problems, everything is okay.

Discussion points

- What does peace mean to you?
- When do you feel peaceful?
- What makes you feel peaceful?
- Can other people make you feel peaceful?
- What kind of people are they?
- Why is peace important?
- List places that make students feel peaceful.
- What color is peace?
- What kind of weather is peaceful?
- What animal could represent peace? Why?
- What sounds are peaceful?

Additional notes

Indicator

- Identifies peaceful places and how to make places more peaceful.

1 Draw a peaceful place and complete the sentence.

I feel peaceful at _____

_____

2 My class and my school could be peaceful if:

_____

_____

_____

Peace – *A peaceful world*

Teacher information

Even young students are exposed to images of war, crime, and violence as they watch television, films, and videos. In the present world climate, teachers should not distress students by dwelling on the possibility of wars within and between countries. Rather, they should emphasize resolving conflicts at all levels to reach a peaceful solution where everyone wins. Emphasize communication and its importance to peace.

Discussion points

- What happens when countries are in conflict?
- What causes countries to argue with each other?
- How can we resolve conflicts between countries peacefully?
- How is conflict between countries similar to/different from conflict between individuals?
- How can we help the world to be a more peaceful place?
- Brainstorm other symbols of peace.
- Learn and invent peace greetings. Practice these in the playground.

Additional notes

Additional activity

- Plant a peace garden, using plants chosen by children from many different countries.

Indicator

- Writes and illustrates a text about peace.

A peaceful world

Below are some symbols of peace.

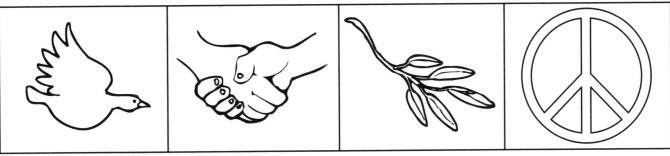

Write a story about peace and draw a picture.

The world would be a peaceful place if _____

_____

_____

_____

_____

_____

_____

_____

_____

Conflict Resolution–Book 1